MARTIN JENKINS and CHARLES ROBERTS

CROSVILLE IN COLOUR 1965-1986

Ian Allan
PUBLISHING

First published 2013

ISBN 978 0 7110 3644 4

Published by Ian Allan Publishing

an imprint of Ian Allan Publishing Ltd, Hersham, Surrey KT12 4RG.
Printed in Estonia

Visit the Ian Allan Publishing website at www.ianallanpublishing.com

Copyright

Dedication

This book is dedicated to the memory of Mike Cozens and Roland Williams, both of whom were passionate about all things Crosville.

PREVIOUS PAGE Mike Cozens often focused on obtaining views in remote, rural locations. This view of dual-purpose Bristol RE ERG284 at Gwenlli crossroads on route S59 from Aberystwyth typifies his patience and his photographic skill. The majority of these well-liked vehicles passed to Crosville Wales on the split of the company in 1986, with the last not being withdrawn until 1989. Many went on to see further service with other operators in the deregulated era. *Mike Cozens*

ABOVE Roland Williams was equally interested in obtaining scenes in out-of-the-way locations, but he also took many views close to his home in Heswall, Wirral, including this winter view of Olympian DOG138 taken shortly after its delivery in 1983. *Roland Williams/Online Transport Archive*

FRONT COVER A superb view of a Bristol VR in classic Crosville surroundings as it approaches Clwyd Gate on the partially limited stop B1X route from Ruthin to Chester via Buckley and Mold in August 1980. At that date DVL433 was just a few months old. *Mike Cozens*

REAR COVER This view, taken in March 1981, typifies Mike Cozens' fascination with tight spots in rural surroundings. Here Bristol LH SLL617 squeezes over a narrow bridge with little clearance on either side as it approaches Nantglyn on route M61 in March 1981. Glan Clwyd was the MAP name given to the revised network in the Deeside and Flintshire area. *Mike Cozens*

Introduction

The Crosville of 1965 had come a long way from its origins as a family firm some 60 years earlier. The company began in Chester in 1906 as a joint venture between George Crosland-Taylor and a Frenchman, Georges de Ville, with the aim of manufacturing marine diesel engines and high-quality cars. The business was a failure, but Crosland-Taylor's sideline of running a fledgling bus service between Chester and Ellesmere Port in 1911 laid the foundation for what would eventually be one of the largest bus companies in Britain. By 1926, the company had expanded into North Wales as well as over much of Merseyside and Cheshire. Its involvement in long-distance coach services also made the Crosville name familiar throughout the country. Then, through a spate of takeovers in the 1930s, Crosville became the dominant presence in the industrial town of Wrexham and gradually a fleet of over 1,000 vehicles, running from over 40 depots, was established.

After the original Crosville Motor Co was acquired by the LMS Railway in 1929, a series of subsequent reorganisations placed it in the hands of the Tilling & British Automobile Traction Co and, in 1942, the Tilling Group, albeit still with members of the Crosland-Taylor family in managerial control. After World War 2, the Tilling Group sold out to the newly formed British Transport Commission (BTC) in 1947 and this move ushered in an era of standardisation on a company that had, since its creation, been highly individualistic and somewhat idiosyncratic. Before the war, the fleet had consisted predominantly of Leylands and, although several batches were delivered until 1950, the principal postwar deliveries were the standard in-house BTC products of Bristol chassis and Eastern Coach Works (ECW) bodywork. Hundreds of Bristol K-type double-deckers and L-type single-deckers replaced remaining prewar types as well as the scores of second-hand vehicles acquired to handle wartime demand. After the last Leylands — a batch of attractive Weymann-bodied PS1s — were withdrawn at the end of 1964, for a brief period the fleet consisted entirely of standard Bristol/ECW combinations until the monopoly was broken by the arrival of two Commer minibuses.

Although many Ls remained, by 1965 the single-deckers had moved on to the underfloor-engined LS and MW, the rather old-fashioned front-engined SC and the rear-engined RE. The first examples of the RE had arrived in coach form for express services in 1963. Double-deckers included some Ks but an ever-increasing number of the innovatively designed Lodekka. The latter was to remain a familiar sight across much of the Crosville network for 30 years.

The 1960s represented a period of gradual decline for the bus industry. Increasing affluence led to higher levels of car ownership and traditional patterns of commuting and leisure travel were taking business away from the industry's core markets. Rising costs, labour shortages and difficulties in industrial relations, coupled with chronic congestion in town centres and along traditional holiday routes, only added to the problems. Crosville's response was to withdraw unremunerative routes and to pursue a much more vigorous policy of conversion to one-man operation (OMO), as a result of which deliveries of new double-deckers ceased for a period after 1968 in favour of high-capacity single-deckers. The industry saw more consolidation of ownership with the Transport Holding Co (the 1963 successor to the BTC) being merged in late 1969 with the newly state-owned former BET Group companies into the new National Bus Company (NBC).

Early in the NBC era, Crosville expanded in two directions. Eastwards, it took over the south and mid-Cheshire operations of the North Western Road Car Co, including their depots at Northwich, Macclesfield and Biddulph, whilst in the south, services and depots were transferred from Western Welsh. In vehicle terms, variety returned in the form of a collection of Leylands, AECs, Daimlers and Dennisses, the fleet already having broken away earlier from Bristol/ECW combinations with a clutch of Bedfords and the ill-fated Seddon RUs.

The creation of NBC also brought about corporate livery changes. Tilling green and cream, in various combinations, had held sway since supplanting LMS maroon in the 1940s, but this was swept away by the ubiquitous NBC leaf green introduced in 1972. Initially unrelieved by any second colour — except on 'local coaches' which were half green/half white — the decision was reversed after a few years and a white band was introduced. The coach fleet, which had been cream and black, took on the NBC corporate all-over white livery, with bold 'NATIONAL' branding, relegating the company name to small letters over the front wheel arches.

The 1970s and 1980s took the company into another era of fleet standardisation, with the Leyland National accounting for most single-deck deliveries between 1972 and 1986, although a small number of Bristol LHs served some of the most rural parts of the network. Under pressure from the Merseyside Passenger Transport Executive (MPTE), new double-deckers entered the fleet from 1975 in the form of the Bristol VR, of which nearly 250 were delivered until production ceased in 1981. Visual variety was provided through a range of eye-catching coach liveries and the use of local fleetnames, which grew out of the NBC Market Analysis Project (MAP).

Historically, Crosville had always been an innovator, mixing and matching bodies and chassis in its long-established Sealand Road Central Works in Chester. The last major engineering project undertaken at Sealand Road involved the transfer of favoured

Gardner engines from scrapped Seddons into Leyland Nationals. Transfers of vehicles from elsewhere in NBC – particularly second-hand (or sometimes third-hand) Bristol VRs – provided some additional fleet variety.

The election of the Conservative Government in 1979 ultimately led to the demise of the Crosville empire. The Transport Act 1985 authorised the piecemeal sell-off of NBC, but as Crosville's size as a single entity was deemed to be bad for competition, the company was split more or less along national lines in the summer of 1986. The result was that a newly formed company – Crosville Wales Limited, with its head office at Llandudno Junction depot – assumed operation for the Welsh side of the company (plus Oswestry) whilst Crosville Motor Services was left with the more densely served part of the former network in Merseyside and Cheshire.

The authors have used 1986 – specifically 25 October, the day before 'D(eregulation)-Day' – as the cut-off point for images in this volume, but a brief chronology of events after that date will provide an explanation for some of the post-1986 events referred to in captions, particularly the way in which the remnants of the company were ultimately partitioned. Crosville Wales was sold to its management team in late 1987 and, although it remained as the same entity through several changes of ownership, it quickly changed its character, with the influx of large numbers of minibuses and second-hand acquisitions, supplanting most of the 'traditional' Crosville types before they were truly life-expired. Crosville Motor Services was sold to the Rotherham-based ATL (Western) Ltd in somewhat controversial circumstances in early 1988 and was then resold to the Salisbury-based Drawlane with suspicious haste. Drawlane, which already had other bus interests in northwest England, set about splitting Crosville between its other companies. Macclesfield and a few smaller outposts passed to the Bee Line Buzz Co; Crewe went to Midland Red North (which later acquired Oswestry from Crosville Wales); Runcorn and Warrington passed to a new North Western Road Car Co, formed in 1986 from the southern part of Ribble's operating territory. Chester, Ellesmere Port, Rock Ferry and West Kirby depots were sold outside the Drawlane group to the Potteries Motor Traction Co (PMT) at which point the sole remaining depot, Northwich, also passed to North Western, and Crosville Motor Services ceased to exist as a company. Later developments brought Chester and Rock Ferry depots into the FirstGroup empire by 1998, and these were resold to Stagecoach in January 2013.

The 20-year period covered by this book revives memories of the final 'classic' period of the Crosville story – an era which took the company from state-owned stability, through the trials and tribulations of the 1960s and 1970s, to the break-up of the mid-1980s and ultimate demise of a much-admired operator coupled with the complete elimination of the Crosville name.

Note on Welsh spelling

The captions in this book use the contemporary – ie 2013 – spelling of Welsh place names; in a number of cases, the spelling of names – such as Caernarvon – was different when recorded in these images.

Acknowledgements

The authors wish to thank all the photographers whose images are shown in the book. Particular thanks are due to Steve Williams for access to the Mike Cozens collection and to Richard Morant for

The Bristol SC was already an old-fashioned design when first conceived, so by the time the last examples were withdrawn in 1976, they looked very anachronistic. Towards the end of its service life, SSG652, resplendent in overall leaf-green, crosses the causeway into Conwy on 8 October 1975 on local service M93 to Pant-y-Tan. *D. Kerrison*

access to the Geoffrey Morant collection. Bill Barlow, Jonathan Cadwallader, Dennis Kerrison and Steve Williams have provided valuable help by checking caption details. Like the authors' previous volume, *The Heyday of Crosville*, this book has been compiled in conjunction with Online Transport Archive (OTA), a UK registered charity established to preserve and conserve transport collections of films, negatives, prints and slides for future generations of enthusiasts. Most of the photographic royalties for this book have been donated to OTA as have the authors' fees.

Bibliography

In researching this book, the authors have accessed a number of publications, most notably *Crosville Motor Services 2* by Duncan Roberts (NBC Books, 1997), *Crosville on Merseyside* by T. B. Maund (TPC, 1992), *The Best of British Buses No 5: – 75 Years of Crosville* by John Carroll (TPC, 1981) and the three-part 'Fleet History' published jointly by the Omnibus Society and the PSV Circle. Further information was obtained from various Ian Allan 'ABCs', Crosville timetables and leaflets as well as personal notes and records.

LEFT The 1972 takeover of routes from North Western took Crosville vehicles over the Cheshire county boundary into Derbyshire. On 15 September 1980, SNL404 is at Canal Street, Whaley Bridge, having worked in on route E24 from Macclesfield. This location was the original starting point of the Cromford & High Peak Railway and its warehouse at the end of the Peak Forest Canal is just out of the picture to the left. The cottages in the background will have been built for canal or railway workers. SNL404 was later one of the 98 Nationals to be given Gardner engines from withdrawn Seddon RUs, the work being carried out at Sealand Road between 1982 and 1985. *Jonathan Cadwallader*

ABOVE At the start of the period covered by this book, the fleet was almost entirely made up of standard postwar Bristol/ECW types from the Tilling/BTC era. The oldest double-deckers were the remaining 7ft 6in-wide Bristol Ks, of which 167 had been delivered in the period from 1946 to 1950. All were fitted with 55-seat lowbridge ECW bodies with a sunken gangway on the offside of the upper deck giving access to rows of bench seats. Orders swapped between AEC and Bristol engines in an apparently random fashion and two of the latter are seen at Rhyl in the mid-1960s. On the left is DKB392 (delivered as MW392) of 1950 and on the right DKB312 (originally MB312) of 1948. Both have the revised front destination display introduced after the 1959 route-renumbering scheme. The two Ks are flanking DLB981, one of six convertible open-top Lodekka LD6Bs delivered in 1959 and painted in the cream and black coach livery for use on the seasonal Promenade services. Here it is loading for Abergele Hospital on the M45. It survived until 1977. *B. D. Pyne/Online Transport Archive*

LEFT Joining the fleet between 1951 and 1953 were 97 lowbridge Bristol KSW6Bs, an 8ft wide and slightly longer development of the K with a Bristol AVW engine. Shortly before its withdrawal, DKB480 (originally MW480 when new) of 1953 is seen parked near Chester Northgate station on 2 May 1967, by which time the top box of the destination display had been painted over. Towards the end of their working lives, older vehicles were often relegated to part-day duties such as industrial or schools workings. For example, the C66 only carried pupils attending Kings, Queens and Holly Bank schools in Chester. *E. V. Richards*

ABOVE The standard postwar Tilling single-decker was the Bristol L fitted with an AEC (L6A), Bristol (L6B) or Gardner (L5G) engine. From 1946 to 1952, Crosville took delivery of various batches of these sturdy vehicles. Dating from 1948, 35-seater SLA77 (originally KB77) was one of the early examples with a 27ft 6in-long body on a 7ft 6in-wide chassis and, when delivered, had destination displays at both the front and rear. It had an AEC 7.7-litre engine and, as on all the Bristol Ks and Ls, a crash gearbox. As part of a drive to cut costs by increasing the use of one-man buses, Crosville converted 41 of its earliest Ls to one-man operation (OMO) during 1957/58, moving the entrance to the front. The driver became responsible for issuing tickets, collecting money and opening and closing the door. During the rebuilding, a new three-section destination display was provided at the front, although the upper aperture was later painted or, as seen here, plated over and the rear display was removed altogether. Strong union opposition to OMO meant these 'converts' sometimes operated with a two-man crew. On 9 July 1966, SLA77 is parked outside Machynlleth station. The following year, it was one of the last four SLAs to be withdrawn. *C. L. Caddy*

LEFT When the maximum dimensions for single-deckers were revised, Crosville took delivery of various groups of LL series buses – the second L indicating 'Long' – between 1950 and 1952. These had 30ft-long 39-seat ECW bodies and were equipped with either Bristol (LL6B) or Gardner (LL5G) engines. During the transitional period around the time wider vehicles were legalised, some 7ft 6in chassis were fitted with 8ft-wide bodies and one of these, SLG200, is seen leaving Wrexham Industrial Estate in March 1968. To cater for those employed on the estate, scores of extra buses were operated on 'workpeople's services' most of which had the prefix 'G'; this was also used in the Wrexham area for routes serving schools, collieries and industrial premises. The G13 operated to Hope some 10 miles to the north. SLG200 was among the last LL-types to be withdrawn in 1970. *A. Mortimer*

ABOVE These two Ls were photographed towards the end of their working lives at King Street bus station, Wrexham on 5 April 1969. On the left is SLG191 (KG191 on delivery) working the D17 to Moss and, on the right, SLB176 (KW196 when new) signed for Tanyfron on the D13. When delivered in 1950, these Ls ha full-width two-section destination displays at the front and rear. The latter was eventually removed totally whilst the front was covered with a panel which reduced the width of the display to allow for standardisation of blinds. With its row of loading bays and concrete passenger shelters, King Street had been Wrexham's principal bus station since 1953 and had, in its heyday, handled up to 1,000 daily departures on a mix of local, industrial, suburban and interurban services. The removable departure boards at the end of the shelters were all produced in the sign-writing shop at Sealand Road. Also using the bus station were some independent operators who had escaped Crosville's voracious takeover policy of the 1930s. When this large site was redeveloped in 2003 a new covered bus station was provided. *Alan Murray-Rust*

ABOVE Crosville's oldest coaches in the mid-1960s were 37 semi-integral Bristol LSs with 39-seat ECW bodies. With underfloor engines, they were classified after the 1958 renumbering scheme CUB (Bristol engines) or CUG (Gardner engines) by the company and were acquired to cater for the booming postwar trade in express coach travel. CUG311 (UG311 when new) of 1953 is seen at the head of a line of buses parked outside Chester Northgate station in 1967. It still retains most of its original body features, including the curved roof lights, wrap-round corner windows and horizontally split windscreen. In the early 1960s, it had been modified with bus-type destination indicators, trafficators, heaters and an electric jack-knife door that had replaced the original outward-opening version. To prolong their active life, many of these LS coaches were converted for OMO in 1967 with driver-operated doors. The following year, they were repainted into dual-purpose Tilling green and cream. CUG311 was withdrawn in 1970. *E. V. Richards*

RIGHT The last seven LS coaches had Bristol engines and the attractive registration numbers SFM 1 to SFM 7. Most, like CUB327 (UW327) shown here, featured a revised design of bodywork that was later to be used on the MW, featuring an inward-opening door. In this view, taken on 12 June 1968, the coach is seen at the seasonal bus station in Rhyl on route M79 to Point of Ayr. Wearing his summer dust jacket, the driver was Llewelyn Williams, a noted bus and railway enthusiast. After being sold in 1971, CUB327 saw limited service elsewhere. *D. Kerrison*

ABOVE Two of the SFM batch received heavy rebuilds during their lives. In 1960, CUB329 (UW329) was returned to ECW where it was rebuilt into a dual-purpose vehicle with a bus-type front section, hinged doors and bus-style indicators. At the same time, the original curved roof lights were removed. On re-entering service as EUB329, it was first painted cream above and green below the waistband. After several subsequent livery changes it was withdrawn in 1970. It is seen alongside a Ribble Royal Tiger in St John's Lane, Liverpool with the south flank of St George's Hall forming the backdrop. The concept of a dual-purpose vehicle able to operate coach duties, excursions and longer stage carriage runs had been adopted by Crosville in 1929. *D. Kerrison*

RIGHT The replacement for the lowbridge K-type was the revolutionary Lodekka. After operating one of the pre-production models in 1953, Crosville purchased another 592 of these 8ft-wide vehicles over a 15-year period. To meet demands for a vehicle that could pass under low bridges whilst having two-and-two seating on the upper deck, Bristol developed the Lodekka with its innovative transmission and drive layout. Accordingly, there was a slightly sunken gangway to the floor of the lower saloon in the low height (13ft 4in), stylish ECW bodies with their rounded front ends and deep windows on both decks. With a bench seat for five positioned against the front bulkhead in the lower saloon, overall seating capacity was 58. By 1961, some 350 of these rugged workhorses had been delivered with either Bristol or Gardner engines. DLB736 (ML736) of 1955 is seen in Lower Bridge Street, Chester, still carrying the 'Long Apron' grille that was originally fitted to the earliest examples. It is on the trunk interurban service D1, which, on weekdays, operated every half hour from Chester to Llangollen with additional journeys on the Chester-Wrexham leg. The bus was withdrawn in 1970 and was sold to Northern General in one of the earliest vehicle transfers within National Bus Company. *Geoff Lumb*

ABOVE Over the years changes were made to the Lodekka design. Compared with the vehicle in the previous picture, DLG890 of 1957 has a shorter length radiator grille and seats for 60. Delivered before the fleet renumbering of 1958 as MG890, it originally had an open platform with rear emergency door but, shortly after entering service, the platform was enclosed and doors fitted. To improve brake cooling, shortened instead of full-length front wings were introduced. Seen heading east from Old Colwyn on the M17 to Llysfaen in the mid-1960s, DLG890 still has its original front destination display. This Llandudno-Rhyl corridor once generated 13% of the company's total revenue with extra buses being drafted in from other depots during the season. After withdrawal in 1973, DLG890 saw further service in the Reading area. *B. D. Pyne/Online Transport Archive*

FACING PAGE TOP Among the 1954 deliveries were eight semi-luxury Lodekkas. These proved especially useful on the company's popular express services linking Merseyside with the North Wales coastal resorts. Painted at first in cream and black with a chrome band between the two decks, ML675-682 (later DLB675-682) had coach-style indicators (later replaced), offside emergency doors, a spacious luggage area, scallop-backed seats for 52 plus tables, and a vending machine in the lower saloon. The extra luggage space was achieved by having a straight staircase, which provided a larger area at the rear, and two removable seats over the nearside wheel arch so that an extra luggage rack could be installed. By 1958, all eight were in dual-purpose green and cream livery (as seen here, although the green roof would later be repainted cream). In the mid-1960s, overall seating capacity was increased to 55 and then, in 1968, they were relegated to ordinary stage-carriage duties and painted into bus green. All were withdrawn in 1971. In this view, DLB679 is in Warrington Arpley bus station on the interurban C30 to Chester. *Geoff Lumb*

FACING PAGE BOTTOM A few Lodekkas had detachable top decks for seasonal use as open-toppers in Rhyl and Llandudno. The earliest examples were eight LD6G 'convertibles', MG811-818 (later DLG811-818), delivered in 1956 with ECW 60-seat bodies. Initially, they were painted in the cream and black coach livery complete with black wings and window surrounds and additional brightwork. In their open-top state, they provided a valuable source of additional revenue when hired out as mobile grandstands, where they offered punters a first-class vantage point for watching the Derby or the Grand National. After making the long journey south, DLG817 is seen at Epsom on 7 June 1972, by which time it had cream window surrounds and a later variant of the upper deck railings with a Perspex screen at the front. The railings and the detachable top decks were held in place by a series of bolts fitted into the strengthened top rail of the body. Shortly afterwards, DLG817 was repainted into all-over NBC green and, as such, played a starring role in one of the film versions of the long-running TV sitcom *On the Buses* starring Reg Varney, Bob Grant and Stephen Lewis. *Alan Snatt*

LEFT Anxious to acquire cost-effective one-man vehicles for use on many of their loss-making rural services, Crosville took delivery of 55 front-engined Bristol SC4LK buses with 35-seater forward-entrance ECW bodies between 1957 and 1961. These lightweight vehicles were underpowered and, as a result, were slow and noisy, especially on hills but, on a long run, their 3.8-litre Gardner engines gave an impressive 20mpg. Although delivered as one-man buses, they did sometimes operate with a conductor. When one-man operated, the driver had to turn round to issue tickets over his shoulder. Initially, the first 16 buses were classified as SC but, after the 1958 renumbering, these, plus the later deliveries, became the SSG class. One of the last to be delivered, SSG678 of 1961, is seen on the forecourt of Machynlleth depot on 31 October 1972. It has just been cleaned and is waiting to be hosed down. The SSGs were withdrawn between 1974 and 1976, with SSG678 being among the last to go. When opened in 1935, Machynlleth depot typified the smaller, more rural type of structures built by the company, that consisted of basic steel frames clad in sheeting. *C. L. Caddy*

ABOVE A total of 24 coach versions of the SC were also ordered. Painted initially in the coach livery of cream and black, these 33-seater CSGs entered service between 1958 and 1960 and were purchased as replacements for the postwar fleet of 47 Bedford OB coaches that had been used mostly in North Wales on local tours and excursions. Hardly ideal for the job, these low-powered vehicles struggled on the steep Snowdonia passes. After a relatively short time, they were downgraded to OMO buses in 1966, when they were given new destination displays and vacuum-operated, as opposed to hand-operated, sliding doors. The new doors proved slow to open and close, thereby elongating running times so the vehicles appeared mostly on lightly trafficked routes or as peak hour extras. Despite being downgraded, they kept their coach classification and seats to the end and could be distinguished by various other features from the saloon version. In this view, CSG662 of 1960 waits at Birkenhead Woodside ready to depart on the F27 to West Kirby on 21 June 1969. When it was withdrawn in 1975, CSG662 was sold for preservation to Dennis Kerrison, a long-standing Crosville enthusiast, many of whose photographs appear in this book. It is now privately preserved in the Preston area. *Alan Murray-Rust*

FACING PAGE TOP Between 1958 and 1966, delivery was taken of 33 Bristol MW (Medium Weight) dual-purpose vehicles with 41-seat, forward-entrance ECW bodies. These were similar to the earlier standard LS saloon but reverted to having a separate chassis. EMG342-356 of 1958 were among the first to carry the new fleet numbers in which the first letter indicated the type of vehicle, the second the chassis type and the third the engine type. These 15 vehicles had bus-style bodies with a notably upright rear end and were originally painted in green with cream window surrounds and waistband. During the 1960s, they underwent several livery changes and EMG355 is seen at Barmouth on 9 July 1966 in cream with green waistband. Eventually, all 15 were equipped for OMO with the loss of two seats. EMG355 was withdrawn in 1976. *C. L. Caddy*

FACING PAGE BOTTOM The 100 MW coaches that entered service between 1958 and 1966 all had Gardner 6HLW engines and manual gearboxes, but three different styles of 39-seat ECW bodies, two of which, both on the X76 to Liverpool, are seen in this view. On the right is CMG469 of 1963, which had the 31ft-long body style first introduced in 1962. This was less curvaceous and had a more upright front than the first body style (which was similar to that shown on CUB329 earlier). It featured a wrap-round windscreen, stepped waistline,

fluorescent lighting, and the Cave-Browne-Cave cooling and heating system. By the time this photograph was taken, in Barmouth on 29 July 1972, it has lost its original curved roof lights, which had been replaced with fibreglass panels. Later, in the mid-1970s, this was one of many earlier MW coaches downgraded for OMO when they were also reclassified as dual-purpose EMGs and repainted in a range of liveries. The coach on the left, CMG556 of 1966, also has a 31ft body but with a deeper windscreen, no stepped side windows, non-opening windows, forced ventilation and, in a style unique to Crosville, an RE-type front grille panel. Although these latter coaches eventually carried out all manner of duties, they were never converted for OMO. CMG556 was withdrawn in 1976 and EMG469 in 1977. *Bruce Jenkins*

ABOVE A total of 103 saloon versions of the MW were delivered between 1959 and 1966, all of which were equipped for OMO. Seen at Machynlleth on 15 July 1971, SMG402 was from a group of seven delivered in 1961. The earlier MW saloons, like this one, had 41 seats including an inward-facing pair over the front wheel arches whilst later batches had 45 forward-facing seats, fluorescent lights and the Cave-Browne-Cave heating and cooling system. SMG402 was withdrawn in 1978, two years before the last of the class. *C. L. Caddy*

FACING PAGE TOP In the late 1950s, there were major improvements to the Lodekka design. These included a virtually flat floor in the lower saloon, air suspension on the rear axle, improved braking – air rather than vacuum – and hopper windows. Four types of these F-series flat-floor Lodekkas were marketed, with Crosville acquiring three of them. Of these, by far the largest group were 127 rear-entrance, 60-seat, 27ft-long FS (Flat Floor Short) examples delivered between 1960 and 1966 with either Bristol or Gardner engines. One of the latter, DFG233 of 1966, is seen approaching Woodside Ferry, Birkenhead on 21 June 1969. It was withdrawn in 1982. *Alan Murray-Rust*

FACING PAGE BOTTOM The next largest group of F-series Lodekkas was represented by the 84 forward-entrance, 30ft-long, 70-seater, FLFs (Flat Floor, Long, Front Entrance) with either Bristol or Gardner engines delivered between 1961 and 1968. One of the earliest, DFB44 of 1961, is seen nearing Heswall bus station on the F23. High-capacity vehicles like this were needed for some of the services linking this dormitory town to Birkenhead, where commuters and shoppers could then travel into Liverpool by railway or ferry. In the Cave-Browne-Cave system – named after its originator, a professor at Southampton University who had served as Director of Camouflage at the Ministry of Home Security during the war – the radiator was located alongside the front destination display with ventilators being provided on either side. The new system also obviated the need for a grille in the usual place and, in this instance, DFB44 has been fitted with a non-standard cowl made in the company workshops. These particular Lodekkas proved heavy and slow, and were disliked by the Heswall drivers. FLFs were familiar sights at many Crosville depots, but unusually not at Wrexham because of union opposition. DFB44 was withdrawn in 1977. *Geoffrey W. Morant*

ABOVE Included among the FLF deliveries were ten superb vehicles built to coach specification and delivered in two groups of five in 1962 and 1964 respectively. Known to the Liverpool crews as 'White Ladies', these striking FLF6Bs had comfortable coach-style seats throughout as well as designated luggage areas within part of the lower saloon; this reduced overall capacity to 55. Sporting the eye-catching cream and black coach livery with sparkling brightwork, one of the 1964 batch, DFB150, is seen in September 1967 in Castle Square, Caernarfon prior to heading for Chester on the through limited-stop 'Cymru Coastliner' L1 service. When introduced in 1965, this was marketed as the 'fast hourly route along the North Wales coast' with a journey time of approximately 3½ hours. In 1968, these fine vehicles were repainted into the green and cream express livery. Latterly, they were often assigned to more mundane duties and were all withdrawn by 1977. *Geoffrey W. Morant*

FACING PAGE TOP Crosville's first two minibuses were delivered in 1964 and, for several years, these Commer 1500s with Perkins engines were the only non-Bristol/ECW vehicles in the fleet. They were acquired specifically to provide partial replacement for loss-making branch-line railways abandoned as part of the Beeching programme of passenger railway closures. One was based at Pwllheli and the other at Bala, where SCP2 is seen in April 1965. Although these operations were financially supported by British Railways, sometimes the only people on board were bus enthusiasts who had often travelled long distances to ride these early minibuses. Painted in dual-purpose livery the bodies, which were converted for PSV work by Harrington of Hove, had seats for 12, a high centre section to the roof, front indicators, a sliding slam-type door and a fold-down step. Of particular interest was the arrangement for turning the indicator and for accessing the roof area. When sold in early 1971, SCP2 saw further use with several other operators. *R. L. Wilson/Online Transport Archive*

FACING PAGE BOTTOM Between 1964 and 1974, Crosville took delivery of nearly 300 Bristol REs. Of these, 47 were RELH coaches with the design of 47-seat ECW body shown here. Built to the new dimensions of 36ft long and 8ft 2½in wide, these comfortable coaches were acquired for major express work and were often assigned to the premier Liverpool-London services. For many enthusiasts these were *the* classic Crosville coach, their only drawback being the offside access to the luggage area that sometimes involved on-street loading. The first 21 RELH coaches had manual gearboxes whilst the remainder were semi-automatic. On 29 July 1967, CRG532 of 1964 was photographed in the cream and black coach livery in Prestatyn bus station on an X41 from Llandudno to Newcastle-under-Lyme. Originally, the four panels on the waistrail displayed 'Crosville - Liverpool - London - Express'; here they have been changed to 'Crosville - Express - Coach - Services'. This particular vehicle was sold in 1980. *D. Kerrison*

ABOVE A total of 46 dual-purpose Bristol RELLs with 50-seat bodies were added to the fleet between 1966 and 1973. Only the first three - ERG593-595 - had the more rounded original style of RE body with narrow entrance door and these were also the only Crosville RELLs with manual gearboxes. On 21 July 1973, ERG595 passes Birkenhead Central Library outbound from Woodside to Meols on the F27. Equipped for OMO from new, the original livery was cream with a green waistband, later cream above and green below the waistband - shown here - and finally the standard NBC dual-purpose green and white. ERG595 was withdrawn in 1980. *G. D. Parry*

LEFT The more upright ECW body style on three dual-purpose RELL6Gs delivered in 1967 – ERG596-598 – is clearly illustrated in this view of ERG596 entering Prestatyn bus station on 29 July 1967. It is working the L1 and has the 'Cymru Coastliner' board attached to the radiator grille. This trio had semi-automatic transmission and, as on the first three dual-purpose RELLs, there were also a couple of little-used luggage lockers located behind the front wheels on both sides. Sometimes, when serving as coaches, luggage was stacked on the front seats or else the seats were folded down to create additional room for cases etc, reducing overall capacity to 44. All three were withdrawn in 1980. *D. Kerrison*

ABOVE Saloon versions of the RE, classified SRG, entered service in quantity between 1967 and 1971. The single-entrance RELLs seated 53, the dual-door 48, and the 33 shorter RESLs only 46. SRG7 and SRG8 of 1967 are of special interest. Their ECW bodies were designed for use on the projected fast, largely segregated Runcorn Busway. The dual-doors were intended to speed up loading and unloading, and the provision of just 30 individual, fibreglass-type seats left ample room for standees. However, both vehicles were reseated for 36 before entering service. This rare view shows SRG7 outside Runcorn depot on 11 August 1967. After being badly damaged by a fire at the same depot in May 1970, it was sent to Sealand Road Works to be assessed for rebodying. However, the decision was taken eventually to dismantle the chassis for spares. The Runcorn depot depicted here dated from 1942. It suffered from structural problems and was replaced by a new depot in 1975. *D. Kerrison*

FACING PAGE TOP In 1968, 10 Bristol RELL6Gs – ERG52-61 – were delivered as dual-purpose vehicles with 50 high-backed seats. Initially assigned to the Wirral area, they were painted cream above and green below the waistrail and originally had reinforced plastic wheel discs, as shown. Although these improved the overall appearance, they were disliked by the maintenance staff and were gradually discarded. On 21 July 1971, ERG54 loads up on route F23 to Heswall at Birkenhead Woodside. The vehicle overtaking it – United Counties No 329 (RBD 329G) – is a bit of a mystery. The photographer remembers being told by the crew that it was on loan to Crosville for experimental purposes, but there has never been any record of this in the history of either company. At the time No 329 was allocated to United Counties' Luton depot, which was, during this period, responsible for covering breakdowns on the M1 for associated companies. As a result, one possible explanation is that No 329 was substituted for a defective Crosville vehicle as no replacement coach was available and Crosville was using it on the F15 before return to Luton. In one of those intriguing coincidences, when Crosville needed a 53-seat single-decker for a school contract in October 1986, it leased the same vehicle from dealers Martins of Middlewich for nearly three years. *J. M. Ryan*

FACING PAGE BOTTOM The 33 shorter RESL6G saloons entered service between 1967 and 1969. All had 46-seat ECW bodies, featuring the first style of flat, shallow RE windscreen. These were among the last buses to have the route number indicator on the nearside. On 28 August 1973, SRG96 of 1969 is seen at Upton Village crossroads on route F35, which linked Birkenhead Park station to West Kirby. SRG96 was withdrawn in 1981. *G. D. Parry*

ABOVE Seen at Conwy on 4 August 1970, SRG137 of 1969 was one of the dual-door RELL6Gs. These high-capacity vehicles had seats for 48 but were also licensed to carry 24 standees for which appropriate strap hangers were provided. The buses had the later design of tall flat windscreen. For ease of operation by the driver, when OMO the route number display had been relocated to the offside. At this time the M22 (Old Colwyn-Conwy) was worked by vehicles experimentally fitted with fareboxes. The orange sign on the front informed passengers that they needed to place their money in the farebox rather than pay the driver. The vehicle was withdrawn in the early 1980s. *Bruce Jenkins*

FACING PAGE TOP Historically, the combined types of Lodekka purchased between 1953 and 1968 formed the largest group of vehicles ever operated by the company. Delivered during 1967 and 1968, and used to replace older Lodekkas at Liverpool, DFG244-263 represented the last batch of traditional two-man, front-engined, half-cab double-deckers to join the fleet. These 20 vehicles had semi-automatic transmission and Clayton heaters. Alongside the last of this batch, DFG263 in Warrington Arpley bus station on 15 August 1970, is DFG192, an FS6G of 1965 complete with the intakes for the Cave-Browne-Cave system. At most times of the day the H2 ran every half-hour to Liverpool with a journey time of 70min, whilst the C30 left hourly for Chester with a time of 67min. The last of this final group of 20 Lodekkas was withdrawn in 1983. *J. M. Ryan*

FACING PAGE BOTTOM Crosville derived considerable additional revenue from the operation of seasonal excursions, especially from the main North Wales resorts where some hoteliers, landladies, traders and shopkeepers acted as Crosville agents. In this role they could reserve places on excursions for guests and visitors. Traditionally, the tours were often advertised on boards propped up against the front of a coach. The Tilling Group decision to allow member companies to acquire some non-Bristol/ECW vehicles enabled Crosville to take delivery in 1967 and 1969 of 14 lightweight Bedford coaches in three distinct batches. The final quartet, delivered in 1969, were Bedford VAM70 with Duple Viceroy 45-seat bodies and the larger Bedford 466 diesel engine. Having helped to transport the crowds to the investiture of HRH The Prince of Wales at Caernarfon on 1 July 1969, these comfortable coaches, with their panoramic windows,

enabled Crosville to compete strongly for the 'tours' trade that was more traditionally the preserve of the smaller coach operator. The last of the batch, CVF694, is seen in Clonmel Street, Llandudno, adjacent to the Crosville Tours Office on 6 September 1972. This style of livery was replaced later by various NBC colour schemes. All four were withdrawn in 1980. *Alan Snatt*

ABOVE Crosville had a long history of acquiring different types of second-hand vehicles. This policy reached its zenith both during and after World War 2, when scores of additional buses were required to meet peak traffic demands. Then, in the mid-1960s, as part of a cost-cutting drive towards OMO, several one-man buses were hired or purchased from other operators. For example, in October 1967, 10 early Bristol MWs were hired from Red & White for a year. When they went back, they were replaced by 10 Bristol LS6Gs purchased from the same company. Painted in Crosville colours and given the fleet numbers SUG282-291, the latter dated from 1953/54 and had 45-seat ECW bodies. They were unusual in having the fuel tanks and fillers on the nearside, and a long stain is clearly visible on this view of SUG288 taken in 1972. Behind is one of three SCs that came to Liverpool to replace double-deckers loaned to Rhyl for the 1972 summer season. During their stay, the SSGs operated as two-man buses covering all manner of double-deck duties for which they were entirely unsuited. The exercise was not repeated. Both buses are on the H9 and are pictured within the Huyton Industrial Estate on the fringes of Liverpool. Withdrawal of the 10 ex-Red & White LSs took place between 1971 and 1973, with SUG288 being one of the last to go. *Peter Jackson*

ABOVE In 1968, Crosville adopted a policy of purchasing single-deckers, although these proved far from ideal when coping with traffic levels on the busier parts of the network. The lightweight successor to the SC was the underfloor-engined Bristol LH, of which 16 were acquired during 1969 and 1970. These 45-seaters had Perkins 5.8-litre diesel engines mounted horizontally midway along the chassis. The first eight were only 7ft 10in wide but the last eight, including SLP156 seen here, were 8ft 2½in wide. Mostly associated with the Wrexham and North Wales areas, this one is seen at Birkenhead Woodside in May 1972. On the left is one of the ventilator shafts for the 1934 Queensway under-river road tunnel. All the SLPs were withdrawn by early 1980. *Alan Atkinson*

RIGHT Crosville became part of the National Bus Co (NBC) on 1 January 1969 but it took some two years before this was fully reflected in the company image. Tilling green gave way to the paler NBC leaf green that became the basis for almost all subsequent bus liveries until mid-1980. The initial NBC specification was for all-over green with no relieving colour, as seen here on DLG806 (delivered as MG806 in 1955) entering Crewe bus station on 3 August 1974. The fleetname and logo were in plain white and all other legal lettering in grey in a font designed specially for NBC. Although the requirements were relaxed fairly quickly, the sight of bland-looking vehicles was to remain a familiar one until the early examples were repainted or disposed of. DLG806 became a driver training vehicle in 1974, receiving a special livery in the process. *Mike Russell*

LEFT The NBC directive for coach-specification vehicles which were not being used on National Express work was for them to appear in 'local coach' livery. In Crosville's case, this meant leaf green and white, as shown on CMG566 complete with fleetname and logo above the saloon windows. This was one of 15 MW6Gs delivered in 1966 with the later version of the Crosville-style ECW 39-seat coach body with no stepped waistrail and no provision for roof quarter lights. They were also the last Crosville vehicles to have slam doors for some 30 years. Seen turning at Chester Town Hall on 13 April 1974 at the start of its journey on the C6 to Overpool, CMG566 is in the company of buses from the City of Chester fleet. CMG566 was withdrawn in 1980. *Alan Snatt*

ABOVE The all-over white livery specified initially by NBC for coaches operating on National Express workings was introduced in 1972, part-way through the delivery of a batch of 10 Leyland-engined Bristol RELHs with a new design of 47-seat ECW body. As a result, the first five entered service in the classic cream and black, whilst CRL264-268 came in white, although the illuminated panel remained with the now-superseded fleetname in black on cream. CRL266 was photographed at Victoria coach station on 30 July 1972. In the early 1980s, the ECW bodied coaches were downgraded for OMO and reclassified, the last example surviving until 1988. *Alan Snatt*

ABOVE Even the luxurious Lodekka coaches succumbed to the all-over green edict. Over the years, they had been gradually downgraded from their original appearance, being repainted green and cream in pre-NBC days, and then into NBC leaf green for regular bus work. Despite this, they still continued to appear on National Express services as well as the 'Cymru Coastliner' for which they remained ideally suited with their sumptuous seats and spacious luggage area - accessed through a door at the rear - at the back of the lower saloon. As late as 31 July 1976, DFB152 was working on the 'Coastliner' and holidaymakers can be seen in Rhyl loading their luggage through the rear door. Even in all-over green, the extra brightwork revived memories of more halcyon days. An interesting comparison may be drawn with the other Lodekka, DFG76, which was, by this time, in the relaxed version of the livery featuring a white band. The different design of upper-deck emergency window on DFB152 was due to the provision of high-back seats with headrests. After being withdrawn in 1977, this former coach served as a staff bus in Gloucestershire; it was then reportedly acquired by travellers and is presumed to have been subsequently scrapped. *C. L. Caddy*

FACING PAGE TOP This unusual colour combination was photographed on 18 April 1974 at Birkenhead Woodside. The previous September, Crosville had secured a contract to transport students to and from Carlett Park College at Eastham, Wirral, for which 11 buses were required. Although the Wirral garages contributed vehicles, additional capacity was needed. As some of Rhyl's 'convertibles' were usually delicensed during the winter months, three, including DLG814 (originally MG814), were relicensed as closed-top vehicles for the Carlett Park contract. The other two were DLG813 and DLG817. Such was the haste with which they were returned to service their roofs remained in pre-NBC colours, resulting in the curious hybrid livery seen here. *G. D. Parry*

FACING PAGE BOTTOM The all-over green edict was also applied to vehicles in the open-top fleet, although they too were subsequently given a white band. However, this combination failed to highlight the tourist nature of the operation. One of the eight 'convertibles' of 1956, again DLG814, was recorded in this uninspiring livery on 3 July 1976 at Bastion Road, Prestatyn, whilst working seafront service M87. DLG814 was not sold until October 1982, having survived long enough to receive the all-over white livery subsequently applied to the open-top fleet. *Mike Russell*

ABOVE NBC continued the Crosville policy of downgrading older vehicles. In the early 1970s, the MW coaches delivered between 1958 and 1961 were equipped for OMO and fitted with bus-type indicators, electrically operated doors and 43 bus seats, some from withdrawn Lodekkas. Colloquially, these conversions were known as 'Crabs' – coaches rebuilt as buses. Painted in bus livery, they were reclassified as SMG and one, SMG413, is seen at Barmouth on the S35 from Blaenau Ffestiniog in August 1972. It carries a short-lived version of the fleetname in large lower-case letters, which was used in 1971/72 prior to the adoption of NBC corporate identity. All of the 'Crab' conversions had been withdrawn from service by 1978, although several went on to have further lives in the Crosville ancillary vehicle fleet. *Bruce Jenkins*

FACING PAGE TOP The Seddon saga has been written about extensively elsewhere. Suffice to say that Crosville, in urgent need of more OMO single-deckers, was allocated 100 buses from a builder new to the mainstream industry: Seddon Diesel Vehicles of Oldham. As a result, 50 RUs with 45-seat dual-door Pennine bodies entered service during 1971; the type was classified SPG. When put to work on the T-series of services

using the Runcorn Busway, they proved unreliable and expensive to maintain, especially as the curvature of the segregated Busway tended to wear out the steering components. Complete with its Busway logo, SPG779 speeds along a 'rural' stretch of the Busway shortly after the first seven-mile section opened on 14 October 1971. Some five years later, the Seddons were replaced on the Busway by older dual-doored REs; these were subsequently replaced by Leyland Nationals. Although a few were converted into single-door vehicles, the Seddons were all withdrawn during the early 1980s. *Peter Jackson*

FACING PAGE BOTTOM The remainder of the Seddon order consisted of 50 dual-purpose vehicles delivered during 1971 and 1972. Some are of the opinion that when compared with an ECW product, the bodies on these 47-seat EPGs had inferior internal fittings, although they did have luggage lockers and kerosene heaters. The overall standard of accommodation proved inadequate, especially when they operated as duplicates on the many express routes serving the North Wales coastal resorts. When almost new, EPG744 is at Wrexham bus station on 5 September 1972 working to the village of Llay. The EPGs were withdrawn between 1979 and 1984. *Alan Snatt*

FACING PAGE TOP Crosville's long association with the integrally-built Leyland National began in May 1972. The National was a joint initiative between NBC and British Leyland, and the result was a vehicle that looked unlike anything else on the market at the time. Its jig-built construction allowed it to be available in two standard lengths – 10.3m and 11.3m – and with a choice of single- or dual-door bodies. All were to have Leyland's 0.510 fixed-head diesel engine. With the potential to be one of the National's biggest customers, Crosville was selected to receive the second production vehicle. Arriving as SNL801, it was initially registered UFM 801K but, on discovering this had already been assigned to an MG sports car in error, it was re-registered WFM 801K. The all-over green was in a different shade from both Tilling and NBC leaf green and SNL801 was also the only Crosville National to wear the pre-NBC fleetname. Here it stands on the forecourt of Chester depot on 1 July 1972. Later the same year, 23 more dual-door versions were delivered with seats for 44 passengers and space for 22 standees, though these came in standard NBC corporate-style livery. SNL801 ran for Crosville until the mid-1980s and, after a period at Gatwick Airport and with Greater Manchester Buses South, passed into preservation. Restored, it currently resides at the Keighley Bus Museum. *R. L. Wilson/Online Transport Archive*

FACING PAGE BOTTOM Crosville eventually had 129 of the dual-purpose 'suburban express' version of the National. Classified as the ENL, these were a marked improvement on the bus equivalent. Employed at first on longer stage-carriage routes or limited stop services like the 'Cymru Coastliner',

they had comfortable seats for 48, strong luggage racks and fold-down seats over the front axles. Eventually, they operated on the full range of services across the network. ENL975 of 1976 is seen in Chester ready to depart on the B4, one of a group of services linking the city with Mold via different routeings. Although initially bearing the Leyland logo on the front panel, this was later replaced by a colour version of the NBC logo. *Mike Cozens*

ABOVE As a result of restructuring within NBC, Crosville's operating territory expanded in two directions in 1972. The South East Lancashire & North East Cheshire PTE (SELNEC) exercised powers granted to it by the Transport Act 1968 and purchased those assets of the North Western Road Car Co within its area. As the remaining part of the company was deemed no longer viable as a stand-alone entity, its bus operations were then split between Trent and Crosville with effect from 1 January 1972, on which date the latter acquired depots at Biddulph, Macclesfield and Northwich, along with 119 vehicles dating from 1957 to 1971, most of which had chassis and body types new to the Crosville fleet. The oldest was North Western No 695, a 1957 Weymann-bodied Leyland Tiger Cub. Crosville's classification system was expanded to accommodate these new arrivals with this type being classified as STL, an unintentional throwback to the classic London double-decker of the 1930s and 1940s. STL901's life with Crosville was destined to be short as it was withdrawn in 1974. On 5 September 1972, it was in Stockport, thought to be on route learning, still with North Western fleetnames but Crosville fleet number plates. *Alan Snatt*

ABOVE Eleven slightly newer 1959 Tiger Cubs – STL906-916 – carried this attractive style of Willowbrook bodywork. On 20 May 1972, STL910 passes through Northwich on the former North Western route E61 to Hartford station. All of the Tiger Cubs were withdrawn by 1976 with most going straight for scrap, although one did survive as an office for two further years, ending its days parked up at Edge Lane depot in Liverpool. *J. M. Ryan*

FACING PAGE TOP The 15 AEC Reliances taken into the fleet from North Western had a mixture of Alexander and Willowbrook bodies. The final four dating from 1963 had Willowbrook bodies with 51 high-back seats for longer-distance services and were received in North Western's dual-purpose livery featuring a higher proportion of cream. In the Crosville numbering scheme they became EAA996-999 and one of these (EAA997) is seen parked at Northwich on 25 March 1972. In spite of the dual-purpose classification, they received bus livery when repainted green. Although the last of these Reliances was withdrawn in 1976, EAA997 succumbed a year earlier and saw service subsequently with operators in North Wales and Liverpool. *J. M. Ryan*

FACING PAGE BOTTOM Crosville also received 13 Marshall-bodied REs dating from 1968 (eight) and 1971 (five). One of the eight earlier short-wheelbase, Gardner-engined batch, SRG230, is at Macclesfield bus station on 5 September 1972 loading passengers for the K38 to Crewe. The depot can be seen in the background. Mechanically, these were identical to Crosville's own REs and, unlike the majority of the acquired North Western stock, later migrated to distant parts of the Crosville empire. They survived in passenger service until 1980/81 with several, including SRG230, being used subsequently as staff buses for drivers taking up duty at Runcorn and Warrington depots. *Alan Snatt*

FACING PAGE TOP Around the time of the takeover, North Western was taking delivery of a batch of ECW-bodied Bristol RE buses that were to a very similar design to Crosville's own but could be distinguished by the detail; for example, the single-piece glass incorporated both route number and destination. The other major difference was the use of Leyland as opposed to the Crosville standard Gardner 6HLX engines, creating the class designation SRL. Five were actually delivered after the takeover in early 1972 and these were built to North Western specification and given their booked Stockport JA-registrations. The very last one, SRL258, arrived from ECW in green and was the only North Western vehicle to have carried the small, all-capital version of the Crosville fleetname rather than the later, larger style. It is seen here at Macclesfield bus station on 5 September 1972. Ex-North Western routes, such as the E8, were incorporated into Crosville's regionally prefixed scheme, the Es having previously been one of a number of series used in the Wrexham area. These later REs operated full service lives, the last not being withdrawn until 1986. After the demise of Crosville, Macclesfield depot went through various changes of ownership until finally being closed by Arriva in 2004. The site has since been redeveloped, Arriva operations continuing from a site elsewhere in the town. *Alan Snatt*

FACING PAGE BOTTOM One unusual feature of the network acquired from North Western was the low bridge under the Bridgewater Canal at Dunham Woodhouses used by buses on route 38 between Altrincham and Warrington. In later years, this had required single-deckers with specially

profiled roofs. As late as 1971, North Western had replaced a batch of Strachans-bodied Bedford VALs with nine Bristol RELLs with dome-roofed 49-seat ECW bodies and one of these, SRL243, by now in standard NBC green, emerges from under the bridge on 17 September 1980. Shortly after delivery, the requirement for these special vehicles was rendered redundant when the bridge was rebuilt in 1972 to a more generous height, but it was still common to see these vehicles assigned to the Altrincham services. The 39 was a peak-hour variant extended to/from the Churchill Works in Broadheath. With a reputation for being less structurally sound than conventional vehicles, these nine buses were scrapped in 1981/82 after 10-11 years' service. *Jonathan Cadwallader*

ABOVE Although North Western's coaching work remained with the rump of the company (soon renamed National Travel North West), a few coaches were acquired by Crosville and initially repainted cream and black. On 11 March 1973, CLL917, one of 11 Alexander-bodied Leyland Leopards dating from 1963 to 1966, backs off the stands at Chester bus station at the start of its journey to Crewe on route K30. When new, these vehicles had operated on North Western's prestigious London services, but with Crosville they were restricted to more local work. By 1975 they had been repainted leaf-green and white and had also been reclassified as ELL and renumbered into the 300s. Four, including ELL317, were converted into recovery vehicles during 1975 and 1976 as replacements for the last surviving Bristol Ls, serving in this capacity until the late 1980s. *E. V. Richards*

ABOVE AND RIGHT One sight associated with the changeover period was similar vehicles in different fleets wearing different liveries. The first view taken on 25 March 1972 shows two Park Royal-bodied AEC Renowns which had been North Western stablemates, but whereas No 964 (right) had become DAA501 in the Crosville fleet, No 122 (AJA 122B) was now in the SELNEC fleet (retaining its North Western fleetnumber), although awaiting repaint into orange and white. Such was the haste with which Crosville repainted its vehicles, Sealand Road Works was unable to cope and some work was farmed out to other NBC subsidiaries such as Ribble and PMT. The experts could spot which vehicle had been repainted where by the slightly different shades of colour. It was quite rare to see a Renown on an express service duplicate, but in the second picture taken on Saturday 27 July 1972, DAA513 is seemingly off-route as it descends the steep hill on Argyle Street South, Birkenhead on an X3 working from Liverpool to Llandudno. During the season, when local depots were unable to supply sufficient vehicles and crews for such workings, it was the policy for other depots to help out and it is possible that the driver, unfamiliar with local geography, may have got lost. The 16 Renowns that passed to Crosville dated from 1963 and were withdrawn between 1976 and 1979, with a few seeing further service elsewhere. Another Renown was acquired for spares from East Yorkshire in 1977. It was rumoured at the time that it was in better condition than the surviving ex-North Western vehicles but permission to put it into passenger service was not sanctioned by Head Office. *J. M. Ryan/G. D. Parry*

ABOVE The Loline was, in effect, a Bristol Lodekka built under licence by Dennis Brothers, in Guildford, at the time when the Bristol could only be supplied to operators in the state-owned sector. During the period from 1960 to 1962, North Western took delivery of 50 with Alexander bodies of which 11 passed to Crosville in 1972 becoming DEG401-411. Carrying the NBC leaf-green livery, DEG407 is in Chorlton Street, Manchester on 7 August 1976 about to return on the E29, one of the trunk routes linking Manchester to Macclesfield. Formerly North Western service 29, it was one of several Crosville services to operate in the SELNEC area. Towards the end of their lives, some Lolines migrated to Warrington depot, becoming regulars on the crew-operated H1 to Liverpool with the last examples leaving the fleet in 1977. Today, the successor organisation to both Dennis and Alexander is one of the country's major suppliers of new buses. *Jonathan Cadwallader*

RIGHT The third and final type of double-decker to enter the fleet as a result of the North Western takeover was the Daimler Fleetline, with Crosville inheriting 19 dating originally from 1963 to 1967. DDG308 was photographed at Cheadle Green en route for Macclesfield on 15 April 1972. Although there are no apparent signs of Crosville ownership on the vehicle, the E-prefix to the route number indicates that the view was taken shortly after the demise of North Western as a stage-carriage operator. The last of these Alexander-bodied ex-North Western Fleetlines was not withdrawn until 1980. *P. J. Thompson (Photosales)*

FACING PAGE TOP In April 1972 Crosville was involved in a further, yet much smaller, territorial expansion that involved the transfer from Western Welsh of seven routes and the depots at New Quay and Newcastle Emlyn – plus an outstation at Lampeter – as well as 11 Leyland Tiger Cubs, all of which were equipped for OMO. The oldest of these was Weymann-bodied STL930 of 1956, which is seen at Newcastle Emlyn on 28 October 1972. Although allocated a number in the main fleet, it only operated briefly in passenger service before being downgraded for use as a towing vehicle when it was renumbered L930. The new classification was achieved by the simple expedient of cutting off the first two letters of the fleetnumber plate with a hacksaw. It retained its red livery until disposal in 1976. *R. L. Wilson/Online Transport Archive*

FACING PAGE BOTTOM Although the ex-Western Welsh buses were all given the same classification, there were numerous differences in the detail. For example, STL934 of 1965 was the only PSUC1/12T variant, the T-suffix denoting the fact that it had a two-speed rear axle for longer-distance work. Although having a Park Royal body shell common with many of the others, it was atypically fitted with 41 high-back seats. In Western Welsh terms, this made it a dual-purpose vehicle so, when it passed to Crosville, it wore this attractive blue and cream livery. It is seen here on 14 July 1973, parked outside New Quay depot; the depot closed in 1976, the year in which the majority of the ex-Western Welsh vehicles were also

withdrawn. Although a 'Crosville' board had been affixed to the depot frontage, the space once covered by the much larger fleetname can still be seen. As STL934 was designated as a service bus by Crosville there were destined never to be any ETL-class vehicles. On repaint, it appeared in the standard all-over leaf green livery. It was disposed of in early 1976. *D. Kerrison*

ABOVE The early repaints of the ex-Western Welsh single-deckers were into Tilling and not NBC green, as seen in this photograph of STL935 taken on 14 July 1973 on the forecourt of Newcastle Emlyn depot; this location doubled up as the boarding point for local bus routes. The bus is on the S44 service from Carmarthen to Cardigan. To aid local passengers, the final digit of the Western Welsh service number was replicated in the new Crosville number; for example, the S44 was previously the 404. Crosville now had a stage-carriage presence much further south than at any other time in its history, but the area included some of the most sparsely-populated parts of West Wales and it was inevitable that, some four years after the takeover, schedules on the S44 would be greatly reduced. Crosville took little time to impose its own identity on this new operating area and within a couple of years, the Tiger Cubs had gone, being replaced by Bristol/ECW types, one of which can be seen on the left. This depot remained a remote Crosville outpost after the splitting of the company in 1986, finally being closed by Crosville Wales in 1990. *D. Kerrison*

ABOVE In the mid-1970s, vehicle shortages were caused partially by the condition of many of the ex-North Western vehicles as well as late deliveries and a shortage of spare parts. Until the situation was rectified by cutting services and acquiring new and second-hand buses, some unfamiliar vehicle types were hired from other operators. For example, during 1974 and 1975, five 1961 Leyland Leopards with well-appointed Harrington Cavalier bodywork came from Southdown Motor Services and were allocated to Crewe, Chester and Macclesfield depots, where they were generally employed on contract work. Although Southdown No 1715 was allotted the number CLL715 by Crosville, this was a paper exercise only, the number never being displayed on the vehicle. During its stay at Chester depot, it was hired by the Crosville Enthusiasts' Club and is seen here at Llanidloes on 15 September 1974. The driver was Eric Manley, a regular for club trips. *D. Kerrison*

RIGHT Also hired from Southdown during 1974 were five Leyland PD3/5s of 1961 with full-fronted Northern Counties 69-seat bodies. As with the Leopards, they retained their Southdown livery, which provided a welcome break from the Crosville leaf green. During the loan period, Crosville classified them as DTO, reviving a classification that had disappeared in 1963, following withdrawal of the company's last PD2s. The quintet spent time at Macclesfield and Northwich as well as at Rhyl as summer extras. The garage foreman at the last-named depot kindly tipped off the photographer that two were scheduled to work one or two evening trips on the M35/M36 circular routes out via Rhuddlan or out via Prestatyn. With part of its front destination display blacked out, DTO632 (Southdown No 932) is seen leaving Meliden on 27 July 1974, working the M36 to Prestatyn. Coincidentally, these circulars had once been a stronghold for the earlier DTOs. A Mini overtakes a Reliant Robin and has the bus in its sights. *D. Kerrison*

FACING PAGE TOP A source of further vehicles for contract work was Western National, more specifically its Royal Blue coaching unit, from which six Bristol MW coaches were hired for some months during 1974. They operated from several depots and one of them, No 2261 (66 GUO), is seen at Chester on 19 January 1974, clearly displaying the obligatory 'On hire to Crosville' sticker. The striking dark blue livery and prominently displayed fleetnames contrasted with Crosville's own MW coaches, which, by this time, had been downgraded to buses and had lost their coach livery in favour of all-over green. *J. M. Ryan*

FACING PAGE BOTTOM Although municipal operators within its area had been introducing Leyland Atlanteans and Daimler Fleetlines since Wallasey's first foray with the former in 1958, Crosville was a late convert to front-entrance/rear-engine double-deck operation. Having adopted a policy of purchasing only OMO single-deckers, Crosville had not intended to buy any more new double-deckers following delivery of the last FLF Lodekkas in 1968. However, responding to demands from the Merseyside PTE (MPTE), which was pressing the company to operate one-man double-deckers, a small batch of nine Bristol VRs was hired from the Potteries Motor Traction Co during 1974 and 1975. Then, in 1975, delivery was taken of 12 new Series

2 VRs with Gardner engines and 74-seat ECW bodies; these were shared between Liverpool, Warrington and Heswall depots. Those allocated to the last named were assigned to routes 418 and 419 that linked Heswall to central Liverpool via part of the M53 motorway and the Kingsway tunnel and formed part of the growing MPTE network of limited stop 'Rapidride' services. Complete with the MPTE 'Rapidride' board at the front, newly delivered DVG266 is at Heswall depot on 16 March 1975. These 12 VRs were withdrawn during 1987 and 1988. *R. L. Wilson/Online Transport Archive*

ABOVE When first introduced, the 'Suburban Coach' variant of the Leyland National provided a very comfortable ride on limited stop services such as the 'Cymru Coastliner'. However, such luxury was arguably of less benefit on routes like Runcorn industrial service J31, which ferried workers from various parts of Runcorn to the ICI Rocksavage Works. Long-serving Runcorn bus ENL940 of 1975 is seen within the works early one Sunday morning. After the change from Local Vehicle Licensing to the centralised DVLC in Swansea, the Crosville tradition of FM-registrations was lost and, for a year or so, it was no longer possible to obtain registrations that matched with fleetnumbers. After 1986, buses no longer penetrated the works. *Chris Palmer*

LEFT The Leyland National was an adaptable vehicle subject to all manner of experiments, one of which eventually involved Crosville. In 1974, Leyland converted Ribble National No 461 (OTF 354M) to battery power by removing the diesel engine and fitting an electric motor, the seven tons of batteries being carried in a four-wheel trailer. At over 13 metres, the unit could not be licensed to run on public roads so, in 1978, it was transferred to Crosville's Runcorn depot for use on the segregated Busway, which was not subject to the length restriction. In a break with tradition, Crosville's classification for this combination was not of the Type-Chassis-Engine format, but XEB, standing for e**X**perimental **E**lectric **B**us. During its stay with Crosville, it retained its NBC red livery and, unusually, its former Ribble number. The experiment was not a success and most known photographs show the vehicle parked up out of use. However, it was hired by the Liverpool University Public Transport Society on 25 November 1978 for a tour around Runcorn and is seen here outside the Weaver Hotel in South Parade, Weston Point, Runcorn. Nominally withdrawn in 1981 and broken up for spares, it had probably not run in service since 1979. It is a salutary indictment of technological development that, some 35 years later, the industry is still no nearer to a practical eco-friendly battery bus. *Andrew Babbs*

ABOVE In a reversal of the long-established policy of downgrading older vehicles, certain types that had been in dual-purpose or bus livery were upgraded in the mid-1970s. The MW coaches were a typical example. Having been in dual-purpose colours since losing its classic coach livery, CMG564 of 1966 had been repainted in National white by 29 July 1978, when it was photographed at Llandudno. Latterly, these MW coaches were sometimes crew-operated on local services, with a quartet from this batch surviving until 1980. After a chequered subsequent life – involving ownership by a scout troop in Wirral and a berry-picking farm in Scotland, and being regarded as a source of spares for a preserved Stagecoach vehicle – sister coach CMG561 has since been restored to its original condition as one of the few surviving Crosville MWs. Crosville's X-series of express route numbers had, by this time, been absorbed into the nationwide National Express series. *D. Kerrison*

LEFT For rural routes where Leyland Nationals were deemed inappropriate, delivery was taken, during 1975 and 1976, of 40 Leyland-engined Bristol LHs. Initially spread widely across English and Welsh depots, they all eventually ended up in North Wales where SLL627 is seen in July 1977 on Porthmadog High Street whilst on route R3 to Blaenau Ffestiniog. Their time in the fleet proved short-lived, with the first of these noisy, lightweight vehicles being withdrawn as early as 1981. Only six remained in stock in 1986 to pass to Crosville Wales. However, with care, their lives could be extended and many former Crosville LHs saw service with Trimdon Motor Services in the northeast of England until the mid-1990s. Three were also exported to Malta, where they served as Route Buses right up until the end of traditional bus services on the island on 2 July 2011. *Mike Cozens*

ABOVE The mid to late 1970s saw changes to the open-top Lodekka fleet. Five of the eight 1956 'convertibles' were withdrawn after the 1975 season and, at the end of the following season, the four remaining 1959 Bristol-engined versions departed. They were replaced by various LDs and FSFs rebuilt to permanent open-top status, some of the work being undertaken at Llandudno Junction depot, where parts including upper-deck railings were taken from withdrawn convertibles. One of the FSFs, DFG81 of 1962, is seen turning out of Clonmel Street, Llandudno on 27 August 1979 in the white livery carried by all open-toppers from 1977. The M17 represented a revival of open-top operation in Llandudno after an absence of many years. Route information was now clearly displayed along each side and there had been an encouraging increase in ridership. The Llandudno open-top operation was withdrawn at the end of the 1981 season and was not reinstated until 1989 by Crosville Wales. *Mike Russell*

LEFT An unusual development occurred in 1977 when DLG944 of 1958 and DLG1 of 1959 were painted white for use, when required, on the Rhyl seafront service, M87. Carrying the appropriate service information, they ran in this form for the whole season. At times they also strayed onto other routes, including occasional forays as far as Liverpool on National Express duplicates or breakdown replacements. On 30 July 1977, DLG1 was recorded on the Rhyl Promenade heading for Pensarn. The following year both vehicles were converted into open-toppers; DLG1 served in this form until the cessation of open-top Lodekka operation in 1983. *D. Kerrison*

ABOVE A small number of elderly LDs survived in the open-top fleet until an advanced age. For example, DLG813 (originally MG813) of 1956 was still going strong on 30 July 1977 when photographed in Rhyl, operating the M87 to Robin Hood Camp. It continued to serve the resort until 1983 when, along with the other remaining open-top Lodekkas, it was withdrawn, to be replaced the following season by OMO open-toppers. Initially, Crosville set this veteran aside for possible preservation and, in 1986, it was still in company ownership when the Welsh part of the business was hived off. Unfortunately, its dateless registration was wanted for a new coach and, as a result, the vehicle was quickly sold for scrap. *D. Kerrison*

LEFT As a swansong, the 14 Bedford coaches delivered during 1967 and 1969 received the National white coach livery in their final years. On 22 July 1977, CVT689, one of the four VAM5s with Plaxton bodywork, turns from Skelhorne Street in order to enter the twin-level Ribble coach-cum-bus station in Liverpool. Much of this scene has changed today, in addition to the traffic flow on the stretch of this road being reversed. The Rail House tower block (right) has been demolished, the St George's Hotel is branded as the Holiday Inn, and the bus station superseded by a development of student accommodation. All 14 Bedfords were withdrawn between 1977 and 1980 after service lives of nine to 12 years, with almost all seeing further service with independents. *D. Kerrison*

ABOVE Well before the fad for small-capacity minibuses in the mid-1980s, Crosville had, as seen earlier, operated two Commer 1500s, which survived until 1971. After a gap of five years, a red-and-white liveried Ford Transit, MTF700, entered the fleet to operate a community bus service in the Corwen area. In 1978, this was joined by MTF701, which had a 16-seat body by Dormobile. It operated service N60 on Anglesey, where it ran down roads unsuitable for full-sized buses. At Beaumaris, connection was made with a service to and from Bangor, on this occasion operated by a flat-screen RE. Painted in NBC dual-purpose poppy red and white livery, MTF701 lasted until 1983, three years before the mass influx of minibuses. *Mike Cozens*

ABOVE Belatedly, a simplified more economical version of the standard Leyland National, known as the B-series, was produced. This was far more suited to rural services and Crosville received the first production example in 1978. Used extensively to replace long-serving MWs, the most obvious external feature was the lack of the distinctive 'pod' at the rear of the roof. One metre shorter than other Nationals in the fleet, they had a seating capacity of 44. In September 1985, SNL589 crosses the Cambrian Coast line at Barmouth. By the end of 1979, Crosville had amassed 85 B-series Nationals, which, along with 264 standard versions (latterly designated A-series), made it the largest operator of this type other than London Country. SNL589 proved to be one of the longest serving. It passed to Crosville Wales on the split of the company in 1986, giving a further 11 years' service before being withdrawn in 1997. It was still in stock when the company was renamed Arriva Cymru the following year, but was already stripped for spares and was eventually sold for scrap at the venerable age of 19. *Mike Cozens*

RIGHT To speed up the MW replacement programme, 13 Bristol LH6Ls were acquired from United Counties in 1978. At first glance these vehicles, which dated from 1969 and 1970, were similar to Crosville's own SLP144-159, but they differed in two fundamental respects: they had Leyland O.400 engines rather than Perkins (hence SLL rather than SLP in Crosville parlance); and semi-automatic rather than manual gearboxes. They had a chequered history with their new owner, with one never entering service and another being badly damaged by fire. Some were even offered on loan to United Automobile Services following a disastrous fire at United's Durham depot in 1979, but they were rejected as the northern operator's LHs were all fitted with manual gearboxes. Shortly after entering service, SLL995 stands at the terminus of the M21 in Coed Pella Road, Colwyn Bay. Regarded as a poor buy, they saw relatively little service and all were disposed of in 1980. *Mike Cozens*

LEFT National Express activity took Crosville coaches all over Britain and they were a regular sight in London on key routes from the northwest. Passing round Marble Arch in April 1974 is Bristol REHL6L CRL293 at the start of its journey to Liverpool on route 850. When delivered in the previous year, this batch of ten Plaxton-bodied vehicles represented a change from standard practice, as all previous Crosville REs had had ECW bodies, and they were destined to remain unique as the following year's order reverted to the Lowestoft-based firm. The ten finished duty on front-line coaching operations in 1981/82 after which they were OMO equipped, reclassified ERL and painted in dual-purpose green and white. As ERL293-302, they were all withdrawn between 1985 and 1987. *Geoffrey W. Morant*

ABOVE An unusual arrival in 1977 was a batch of 10 1962 FLF6Gs from the Bristol Omnibus Co that directly and indirectly allowed for withdrawal of the last of the ex-North Western Lolines and Renowns. Initially on loan, two of the vehicles were returned to Bristol, whilst one of the remaining eight, although purchased, was never used. The remaining seven saw service at a number of depots. The most noticeable external difference from Crosville's own Lodekkas was the T-shaped destination display. DFG746, formerly Bristol No 7046, was based at Mold and is seen at Pantymwyn on 23 February 1980. Operating every two hours, the journey time from Birkenhead Woodside was just under 90min. In the early postwar years, this service had been especially popular at weekends with Merseysiders escaping into the Welsh countryside and duplicates were often needed. Acquired as a short-term expedient, all seven were withdrawn by the end of 1980, although one had a second life as a project office in connection with the Market Analysis Project (MAP). *Jonathan Cadwallader*

ABOVE Although a late convert, Crosville acquired 243 new VRs, all with 74-seat ECW bodies, between 1975 and 1981. DVL321 was one of the early examples fitted with the Leyland O.501 engine, a vertically configured version of the engine fitted to the Leyland National. It is seen here at the picturesque West Wirral village of Parkgate in August 1983 that, in times past, had been a more significant port than Liverpool. The silting of the River Dee created the now familiar marshes and the incongruous sight of a sea wall a considerable distance away from water other than on occasions of the highest tides. The narrow road skirting the riverbank required vigilance on the part of drivers, particularly in foggy conditions, when legend has it that on at least one occasion, a driver steered his bus down a former slipway onto the marsh itself. *Jonathan Cadwallader*

RIGHT Early VR deliveries were assigned to the more urban parts of Crosville's territory but, as the type became more widespread, they could be seen across the network. A few years after delivery, the highest numbered DVL in the fleet, DVL499, passes through the Cheshire village of Church Minshull whilst running on the K31 from Winsford to Crewe. Although Crosville had standardised on Gardner engines for its later VRs, DVL499 was one of a 1979 batch of 14 to be fitted with the less successful Leyland O.501 because of production problems at Gardners. Although the Leyland engine gave good acceleration and a higher top speed, it also caused considerable maintenance problems. *Mike Cozens*

FACING PAGE TOP As already mentioned, the Seddon RUs proved problematic, requiring a significant amount of rebuilding. One outward sign of the work was the cutaway skirt at the front, which avoided the grounding problems to which they had originally been susceptible. During 1977 and 1978, ten were rebuilt for service in North Wales with single doors and seats for 51 passengers. Withdrawals began in 1980, when the vehicles were only nine years old, although a few did survive until 1984. Their demise was hastened in part by a decision to recycle their Gardner engines into a significant number of Leyland Nationals. On 6 September 1982, SPG764, one of the ex-Rhyl single-door conversions, was photographed in the attractive Shropshire market town of Ellesmere. *Jonathan Cadwallader*

FACING PAGE BOTTOM As part of a successful compensation claim against Seddon Motors, Crosville was given an additional vehicle free of charge in 1974. At first glance it appeared similar to the other Seddons but was in fact one of the company's Pennine 7s that incorporated a mid-engine rather than the rear-mounted unit in the RUs. Having served briefly as a demonstrator it was, despite being built to dual-purpose specifications, given the Crosville fleet number SPG699. Intended to compete with the Leyland Leopard, the design achieved reasonable market success, with many entering service with Scottish Bus Group subsidiaries until production ceased in 1982. However, SPG699 was the only example in the NBC fleet and spent its entire life at Chester depot until withdrawn in 1986. Although mostly assigned to Chester locals, it was occasionally used on longer-distance services and is seen here on the limited-stop service L2 at Beeston in September 1983. *Mike Cozens*

ABOVE By 1980, the dwindling number of Lodekkas were confined to a few depots, one of which was Liverpool where they still worked on a number of busy routes. For many years, lines of these vehicles could be seen double-parked on Mann Island, Liverpool, waiting to take up service. In time-honoured fashion, the conductor of DFG206 adjusts the blinds before departure on route 76 heading for Prescot, in the company of earlier FSF DFG62 dating from 1961. Operation of the 76 had been transferred to Crosville by the MPTE in October 1973, which explains its exclusion from the Crosville H-series of route numbers. Until withdrawal of the last Lodekkas on 29 March 1981, the 76 and the H1 were the last crew-operated routes in the Merseyside area. In the background is the famous White Star building from where the sinking of the *Titanic* was announced in 1912. Most of the buildings on the right-hand side have been replaced in recent years by rather unattractive structures that detract from the traditional architecture of the area. *Jonathan Cadwallader*

FACING PAGE TOP Until September 1981 Wrexham remained another Lodekka stronghold. A few months earlier, DFG236 arrives at King Street bus station on the long D1 route from Chester to Llangollen. NBC instigated the Market Analysis Project (MAP) in the late 1970s, resulting in some significant service revisions in the shire-county parts of Crosville's empire in 1980 and 1981. Allied with this, a series of local brand identities was introduced that largely supplanted the Crosville name; the 'Wrexham' branding is clearly shown here. *Roland Williams/Online Transport Archive*

FACING PAGE BOTTOM When finally displaced from their original stamping grounds at Merseyside and Cheshire area depots, many of the last batch of Lodekkas – the 20 semi-automatic FLF6Gs of 1967/68 – gravitated to Bangor mainly for schools services. This rear-end line-up shows eight of the vehicles at the back of the depot in 1981. Other than the open-top fleet and a few special events, traditional half-cab operation ended in 1983. For many years, Bangor remained as the principal depot in northwest Wales, but was eventually closed in 2005 and the land sold for redevelopment, with operations moving elsewhere in the city. *Roland Williams/Online Transport Archive*

ABOVE Crosville continued with its long-standing policy of downgrading and reclassifying coaches once their days on frontline service had come to an end. As the last coach to be delivered in cream and black livery, CRL263 of 1972 had been allocated to Edge Lane depot in Liverpool for the London services. In early 1980, it was equipped for OMO and emerged in dual-purpose livery as ERL263 and is seen here at Machynlleth on 10 November 1980 on a temporary railway replacement service. It was withdrawn from service shortly before the 1986 partition of the company. After being used by Gloucestershire County Council as a mobile technology unit for seven years, it returned to passenger service with the Northern Bus Co of Sheffield, but was damaged in an accident shortly afterwards and sold for scrap in 1995. *D. Kerrison*

FACING PAGE TOP Starting in 1979, Crosville took delivery of 56 Leyland Leopards, the majority with Duple Dominant II bodies. These came as both coaches and dual-purpose vehicles, with the latter being equipped for OMO. In reality, there was often very little distinction between the two. The 1979 order for Duple-bodied Leopards arrived as a mixture of ELL and CLL, and two even had their designation changed before entering service. Although ELL506 was one of those classified as dual-purpose, it is seen inside Skelhorne Street bus and coach station, Liverpool, on 10 July 1982 operating a National Express duty to London on route 850. After the split in 1986, ELL506 remained with the English part of the company but was withdrawn after just a couple of years' further service and sold to SUT, a post-deregulation reincarnation of Sheffield United Tours, that ran quite a number of ex-Crosville vehicles at that time. *Jonathan Cadwallader*

FACING PAGE BOTTOM One of the most spectacular routes was the R40 to the Stwlan Dam, which attracted both tourists and bus enthusiasts alike. The buses climbed high up above Blaenau Ffestiniog to the upper dam, part of a pump-storage electricity generation scheme. As the section up to this dramatic location was on a private road, the driver was provided with a key

to open and close the gate before making the twisty journey up the steep gradient to the dam itself. On 12 June 1982, Bristol LH SLL627 has just dropped off its passengers, who are admiring the rugged scenery. *Charles Roberts/Online Transport Archive*

ABOVE The classic RELHs with ECW coach bodywork soldiered on into the 1980s, with some being downgraded to dual-purpose. However, the earlier manual-gearbox examples were deemed to be unsuitable for this purpose and were all withdrawn by the end of 1980. One of these, CRG575, last saw service on a snowy 23 March 1980 and was caught on film literally during its final hours. Having been hired by the Merseyside Bus Club for a tour, it had come from Crewe depot and was driven by Geoff O'Brien. After picking up passengers outside Liverpool Central station, it was tackling the hill approaching Skelhorne Street bus and coach station when it suffered a transmission failure and is believed never to have run again. The illuminated fleetname is very apparent on this snowy spring morning. Originally there were four illuminated panels but, in 1972, all but the fleetname were removed. Several of these popular vehicles, in both manual and semi-automatic forms, survive in preservation. *Charles Roberts/Online Transport Archive*

LEFT Many older REs were withdrawn during the early 1980s, including the small batch of dual-purpose RELLs delivered in 1968. Latterly allocated to Oswestry, ERG60 is seen approaching the town centre in April 1980, having just travelled from Black Park (near Chirk) via Weston Rhyn, in spite of the destination for the outward journey still being displayed. Three of this batch were initially preserved, but sadly ERG56 was subsequently destroyed in an arson attack in Pensby. More happily, ERG52 forms part of the Wirral Transport Collection in Birkenhead and, fully restored to its original livery, is housed at its premises in Taylor Street. *Roland Williams/ Online Transport Archive*

ABOVE SRG69 was one of the 10 dual-door RELLs delivered in 1968 and 1969 that, when new, were split between Wirral and Chester depots. Their centre exits were never really used to full effect, the majority of drivers preferring to control passenger flows through the front door. By September 1980, SRG69 was allocated to Ellesmere Port, which had depot status but no designated facilities, vehicles being parked in the bus station and being dispatched to Chester for maintenance. As part of the MAP initiative described earlier, the Ellesmere Port network of routes was rebranded 'TransPort' in 1980, with the small windscreen on the RELLs providing sufficient space for this new fleetname to be squeezed in above the destination box. The F66 was a cross-town route linking Wetherby Way and Stanney Grange, and had been OMO since 1969. SRG69 was withdrawn shortly after the date of this photograph. *Roland Williams/Online Transport Archive*

For the launch of the Mid-Cheshire MAP scheme in 1980, SNL386 was painted in an attractive blue and cream colour scheme, intended to replicate that of the former Mid-Cheshire Motor Bus Co. In the 1920s, Crosville and North Western had competed to buy this business and it was the latter's successful purchase that had given it a substantial presence in that part of the county. Pictured at Northwich in 1980, SNL386 remained allocated to this depot right through until the split of the company, when it passed to the new North Western company in 1988. To promote the new network, it originally worked on all the local routes at a flat fare of one penny. *E. V. Richards*

Leyland introduced a new version of the National in 1979, designated the National 2. Many of the features of the original type were retained, but the radiator was moved to the front of the vehicle resulting in a much more rounded appearance. The trouble-prone 500-series engine was dropped, being replaced by the Leyland TL11 engine that was a development of the O.680 as used in Crosville's Leopards. Five National 2s were delivered each year between 1981 and 1983, all being to dual-door specification for Runcorn Busway services. Because Crosville's fleet numbering had become slightly chaotic, their numbers reverted to the beginning of the sequence. The first of the batch – SNL1 – is seen at the head of a line of vehicles parked out of service on the Busway during the occasion of an open day held at Runcorn depot on 17 July 1983. The special Busway livery, with an orange band featuring a stylised 'T' (Busway services were all numbered in the T-series), was introduced in 1982. The registration AFM 1W unintentionally harked back to Leyland Cub N106 of 1935 that had been registered AFM 1, the first three-letter registration issued by Chester. Changing requirements after deregulation in 1986 meant these vehicles had only relatively short lives. Several, including SNL1, were heavily rebuilt by East Lancs to its Greenway specification, after disposal.

Roland Williams/Online Transport Archive

ABOVE Older vehicle types also received the T-livery, including SRG143, seen here on the Busway in Runcorn Old Town on 27 March 1982. The bus also bears a non-standard black front grille, presumably to make it similar, at first glance, to the National 2s. As originally envisaged, the Busway was to have only been used by Runcorn town services, with passengers transferring onto interurban routes at a twin-level interchange at Shopping City. Gradually this philosophy was diluted, as illustrated by the following dual-purpose National that was on the H25 to Liverpool. The Busway remains in operation today, although some short sections, including the one shown here, have now been redesignated for general traffic use. *R. L. Wilson/Online Transport Archive*

RIGHT From 1980 onwards, Crosville accelerated its policy towards double-deck OMO by acquiring second-hand vehicles from other operators. Most came from other NBC subsidiaries, although the first six were ex-South Yorkshire PTE and formed part of a batch of Series 2 VRs with Gardner engines new in 1972 to Sheffield Corporation and painted originally in the corporation's attractive cream and blue livery. Unlike Crosville's own ECW-bodied examples, they were fitted with East Lancs 73-seat, highbridge bodies, which limited their usefulness in the fleet. They were initially allocated fleet numbers DVG11-16 – the reason for these totally out of sequence numbers is not known – but before entering service it was decided to bring in a new category of vehicle – H for Highbridge – so they became HVG11-16 instead. Following a staff suggestion that Crosville adopt City of Oxford Motor Services' policy of numbering highbridge vehicles in the 900s, they eventually became HVG931-936, following on from the ex-Southdown Fleetlines (which arrived a few months later), with the result that HVG936 had the distinction of being renumbered twice before it had even entered service. At the time of the company split, HVG932, shown here, was the only one of the six vehicles still in stock. Latterly it operated a free bus service from Ellesmere Port to an Asda supermarket in Birkenhead and is seen here passing along Conway Street on 15 May 1984. It was withdrawn shortly afterwards. Although most of the buildings behind the bus were demolished to make way for Europa Boulevard and Conway Park railway station, at the time of writing The Crown pub remains open for business. *Charles Roberts/Online Transport Archive*

ABOVE In 1980, 30 Daimler Fleetlines dating from 1970 to 1972 arrived from Southdown Motor Services. The first 15 were Gardner-engined and fitted with Northern Counties bodywork, becoming the HDG class and, at first, were mainly allocated to Wrexham, where they ousted some of the last Lodekkas. In early 1984, six were converted to open-top form to replace the remaining open-top Lodekkas at Rhyl. They were outshopped in a two-tone green and white livery based on colours used on some Crosville coaches around the same time and inspired by the National Express 'Venetian Blind' livery that had recently been introduced. The six buses were also given names, believed to have been the first time Crosville had done this since before World War 1. HDG908 bore the name *Criccieth Castle* on the nearside and its Welsh equivalent, *Castell Criccieth*, on the offside. It is seen in Rhyl on a bright, sunny 22 July 1984. These Fleetline open-toppers were withdrawn by Crosville Wales in 1994/95. *D. Kerrison*

RIGHT The other 15 ex-Southdown Fleetlines had Leyland engines – hence the designation HDL – and ECW bodies, broadly to the same design as Crosville's own VRs. The cluster of routes east of Caernarfon took vehicles into some very dramatic Snowdonia scenery. On a bitterly cold day in early 1981, HDL924 is seen approaching Dinorwic quarry on route N93 from Caernarfon. The Fleetlines were not renowned for good road-holding and the sprinkling of snow would have made the driver even more cautious than usual, especially if the surface was also icy. Along with the closed-top ex-Northern Counties Fleetlines, the HDLs were all withdrawn in 1986. *Mike Cozens*

FACING PAGE TOP To add to their own 243 ECW-bodied VRs, the company acquired a further 42 from elsewhere in NBC in the period from 1981 to 1985, including several that had unusual pedigrees. DVG552 was new to Scottish Bus Group subsidiary Alexander Midland in March 1970. Difficulties with operating this type of vehicle in Scotland led to an exchange of VRs and late-model Lodekkas between the SBG and NBC, as a result of which this vehicle ended up operating for Eastern National in Essex. Withdrawn by Eastern National in 1982, it passed to Crosville and is seen here in Tyn-y-Morfa in early 1983. Already 17 years old at the time of the splitting of the company, it ran with Crosville Wales until early 1988. *Mike Cozens*

FACING PAGE BOTTOM East Midland provided batches of VRs in 1982 and 1984. DVG568 came in the first tranche and is photographed at the holiday village of Borth, near Aberystwyth, on a rather windswept day in the late summer of 1985. The S12 connected Aberystwyth to Tre'rddol. When withdrawn by Crosville Wales in the late 1980s, this bus saw further service with a Cheshire-based independent. *Mike Cozens*

ABOVE As well as second-hand purchases, Crosville hired various vehicles during the mid-1980s to cover specific requirements. Within the Merseyside area, Crosville's mileage was operated under contract to MPTE, which wished to increase the proportion of OMO double-deckers. As a result, 10 MPTE MCW-bodied Fleetlines were loaned to Crosville for use at its Heswall depot. Painted in full NBC livery for the duration of the hire, three can be seen in this view on the approach to Birkenhead Woodside, with the Mersey Railway pumping station building as a backdrop. To the fore is HDG939 (No 3019 in the MPTE fleet), with its blinds set for school service 611. The hire lasted for approximately a year but, later, some of the batch had a further period with Crosville. Surplus to PTE requirements at deregulation, a large number – including No 3019 again – were again hired by Crosville to operate tendered services. Thereafter, many were sold to Gold Star Coaches in St Asaph, an operator that also established an operating centre in Birkenhead trading as Busman Buses, where this time No 3019 ran in competition with Crosville. *Mike Martin*

ABOVE Vaggs Coaches of the quaintly named Knockin Heath in Shropshire was a long-established independent family firm, having been founded in the 1920s, which latterly had licences to services in the Oswestry and Shrewsbury area. Faced by mounting losses, the company went into liquidation in September 1982 and Crosville was called upon to provide some of the replacement services with the V-series being used for the routes taken over. This letter had never previously been used, the last addition being the Ts for the Runcorn Busway. Among the mixed bag of older vehicles drafted in was SNL816, which was 12 years old when photographed outside The Bridge Inn at Ruyton-XI-Towns on 24 May 1984. *Charles Roberts/Online Transport Archive*

FACING PAGE TOP Crosville's last new batch of Leopards were 15 Willowbrook-bodied examples, all of which required major structural modification before entering service so they were significantly behind schedule when delivered during 1981 and 1982. As a result, their planned fleet and registration numbers were voided and they entered service as ELL20-34. They were delivered in a variety of combinations of NBC green and white but were all repainted into the version shown here on ELL28, which is seen on William Brown Street, Liverpool, on 24 March 1982

probably having just dropped off a visiting school party. The colours were similar, but not identical, to those that had first appeared on the Town Lynx vehicles between Flint and Manchester Airport in 1979. This livery represented the first major break from NBC uniformity by the company. Passing to Crosville Wales at the split, ELL28 lasted only until early 1987, being one of a number of this batch to run subsequently for the well-known northeast independent OK Motor Services. *Jonathan Cadwallader*

FACING PAGE BOTTOM Although the Willowbrook-bodied Leopards were not highly regarded from a build quality point of view, that did not prevent several being upgraded for National Express work and fitted with toilets for use on the Irish services using the ferry crossing at Holyhead. In this view, however, ELL24 is on one of the interurban routes linking Holyhead and Bangor. As a full-specification coach, it would have been reasonable to expect it to have been a CLL by this stage, but this batch of vehicles was characterised by inconsistent reclassifications during their time with Crosville. The last were finally withdrawn by Crosville Wales in 1994. Many lasted just seven years before disposal, including ELL24, which was one of three to later run for Grimsby-Cleethorpes Transport. *Mike Cozens*

ABOVE In 1982, a pair of Duple-bodied Leopards acquired from Ribble was added to the dual-purpose fleet. They were from a batch delivered in 1973/74 and later converted for OMO. Although acquired by Crosville for relatively local work, it was not unusual for them to venture further afield and ELL524 is seen turning from Semley Place into Victoria coach station to pick up passengers at the start of its long journey on route 853 from London to Holyhead. *Geoffrey W. Morant*

RIGHT The Leyland replacement for the Bristol VR was the Olympian. Crosville was one of its early NBC customers, with 112 eventually entering service between 1982 and 1985. There was a suggestion at the time that they might have appeared as DLG class, but the company stuck with logic and designated the bulk of them as DOGs. One of the first batch, DOG105, is seen passing Upton Convent on 9 September 1982 en route for West Kirby, a few months after entering service. In 1979, Crosville's Wirral routes had been recast and fully integrated into the Merseyside PTE network, with the 81 and 82 linking Birkenhead, Woodside to West Kirby by different routes, which together provided a 15min headway between the two termini. This vehicle passed to PMT when it acquired the Wirral and Chester operations of Crosville (England) in 1990. *Charles Roberts/Online Transport Archive*

ABOVE The final 13 Olympians were specified with coach seats for operating on particular routes and, with a break from tradition, were classified EOG, using a prefix that had hitherto been limited to single-deck dual-purpose vehicles. EOG203 was one of 10 vehicles allocated to the 'Cymru Coastliner' in March 1986 and is seen two months later outside Llandudno Junction depot in a new eye-catching livery incorporating the colours of the Welsh flag and resplendent with a Welsh dragon on either side. The places served were also picked out in red. At the split of the company, it was initially planned that both parts of the company would work on the 'Coastliner' and, being based at Chester depot at the time, EOG203 was allocated to the English part of the company. A change of plan saw the entire operation pass to Crosville Wales, with the result that this vehicle passed between the two companies, the only bus ever to do so. Olympians remained with Crosville's successor companies into the early 2010s. Two EOGs have been preserved. *Mike Martin*

RIGHT Two well-appointed Leyland Royal Tiger coaches with semi-integral Roe Doyen bodies were delivered in 1984, initially for an ill-starred programme of overseas holiday tours titled Euro-Lynx International for which purpose they had a special livery, toilets, videos and a hot drinks machine. After a period serving as team coaches for Chester and Wrexham football clubs, the pair was used for National Express work and CYL430 is seen climbing away from Birkenhead, Woodside en route for Liverpool on route 361 in 1986. Both were withdrawn by Crosville Wales in 1988 and went on to have a succession of owners in the independent coaching sector. Following the fashionable trend, from new they carried cherished registration numbers donated by Bristol MW recovery vehicles built from two of the 'Crab' conversions described earlier, and these same numbers subsequently reappeared on a pair of Dennis Javelins new to Crosville Wales in 1988. *Mike Martin*

LEFT When production of the Leopard ended, Crosville's preferred choice of coach chassis became the Leyland Tiger, with 33 examples entering the fleet in the period between 1983 and 1986. All but the first pair were bodied by Duple, but to three different designs. The final 15, delivered in April 1986, had the 340 style of bodywork, although to several different specifications depending on the type of intended work. Destined to be Crosville's last new coach, CTL77 was one of three delivered to National Express's 'Rapide' specification and is seen here in the appropriate livery in Llandudno in September 1986. Seven of the coaches (including CTL77) passed to Crosville Wales where they were withdrawn between six and 13 years of age. Those with the English company were withdrawn with unseemly haste on privatisation of the company in 1988 but quickly found their way onto the second-hand market.
R. L. Wilson/Online Transport Archive

ABOVE Except for the small-scale operation of Ford Transits in the 1970s, as described earlier, Crosville was slightly later than some NBC operators in starting minibus operation. The first examples, delivered as part of the mass introduction of the type across the industry, were six Mercedes-Benz L608Ds converted from vans by Reeve Burgess. These 20-seaters arrived at Sealand Road early in 1986 and two, including MMM708, are seen inside the works before entering service in their original Mini-Lynx livery. Initially they saw very little use with Crosville. After spending time in storage, in October 1986 they went on loan to Alder Valley for about a year before entering service in a different livery. They were withdrawn during 1989 and 1990. *Mike Martin*

ABOVE A further sign of impending deregulation was a stipulation by Gwynedd County Council that all vehicles operating on its subsidised services should incorporate the predominant red and yellow 'Bws Gwynedd' branding at the front of their operator's livery. Just months before deregulation, on a wet 12 April 1986, SNG415 loads up with passengers in Blaenau Ffestiniog on route R35 for Dolgellau. The SNG classification denotes that this was one of the 98 Nationals to be converted to Gardner power by using refurbished and uprated engines taken from the unsuccessful Seddon RUs. SNG415 had only been converted in March, making it one of the last to leave Sealand Road Works where activity was now winding down pending final closure in 1988. *D. Kerrison*

RIGHT During 1986, more signs of pending change became apparent. For example, DVL352, a 1977 VR, was one of the first vehicles to be painted in a dark green and orange livery for the English side of the company and is seen shortly after this repaint on 11 October 1986 in West Kirby. Straddling the partition date, about 30 buses of various types were painted in this livery before the decision was taken to replace the brash marigold orange with a more sombre cream. It is a testament to the photographic legacy of the late Reg Wilson that a picture of Crosville Bristol K taken very close to this location appears under his name in the 1966 Ian Allan *Crosville ABC*. *R. L. Wilson/Online Transport Archive*

At first glance, the last image in this book seems unremarkable. It was taken on 20 September 1986, just a few weeks before D(eregulation)-Day and shows a leaf green National operating in traditional Crosville territory. On closer examination, the NBC logo on the front of SNG408 has been painted over, leaving just the plain Crosville fleetname – a sign of things to come. However, even then it would have been hard to predict that, within four years, Crosville would, to all intents and purposes, cease to exist. The English side of the company was broken up and sold off on a piecemeal basis and the name Crosville eventually dropped as a brand. Crosville Wales did continue under a variety of different ownerships but was eventually subsumed into Arriva, as, ironically, was a portion of the English operations. Today, there are now many people across the former Crosville network who have never heard of the company and know little of the origins of their remaining bus services. It is hoped the photographs selected for this book will help to keep the Crosville name alive and also recapture something of the special appeal of this remarkable operator. *R. L. Wilson/Online Transport Archive*